**Not In So Many Words:
Poems & Commentaries on Poems**

Not In So Many Words:
Poems & Commentaries on Poems

The Poetry Business Writing School 2002–2004

Smith/Doorstop Books

Published 2005 by
Smith/Doorstop Books
The Poetry Business
The Studio
Byram Arcade
Westgate
Huddersfield HD1 1ND

Copyright © The Contributors 2005
All Rights Reserved

ISBN 1-902382-69-2

British Library Cataloguing-in-Publication Data. A catalogue record for this book is available from the British Library.

Designed and typeset at The Poetry Business
Printed by Antony Rowe, Chippenham

Distributed by Central Books Ltd., 99 Wallis Road, London E9 5LN

The Poetry Business gratefully acknowledges the help of Arts Council England and Kirklees Cultural Services.

CONTENTS

Introduction

9   Sally Baker: 'Mytholmroyd Giant'

13   Susan Burns: 'Friday Night At The Travellers'

19   Chris Considine: 'Dr Feldheim's Calendar'

23   Peter Knaggs: 'Spiderlings'

27   Kath McKay: 'Menu del Día'

31   Paul Mills: 'The President of England'

35   Jane Routh: 'The River Pilot's Wife'

39   Ann Sansom: 'St. Augustine's House'

43   John Siddique: 'Other People's Children'

47   Steven Waling: 'You Showed Us Your Row Of Cups'

51   Sue Wood: 'The Craft of Spines'

55   Cliff Yates: 'Hôtel de l'Angleterre'

Notes on Contributors

INTRODUCTION

We hope you will agree that these poems, together with the commentaries, make fascinating reading. What is so good from our point of view is that the commentaries are both entertaining and extremely practical (considering what scope there is in such a project for disappearing up one's own critical apparatus). But the essays were after all written by practising poets rather than academics or aestheticians, and what's more by poets from the North of England; and though there isn't a great deal of theorising here, there is plenty of insight into the creative process.

The Writing School was set up in 2002, with the support and encouragement of the Arts Council England (Yorkshire). It was felt that there are a number of avenues for new writers, but that once you are under way as a published poet it's almost impossible to find the kind of help and direction that most of us need. The idea arose to provide a structured learning experience for just such poets, based on MA modules which Peter taught for ten years, but tailored to the needs of a small group of people well able in a very real sense to work together.

Over eighteen months, the dozen poets featured here wrote and shared their work. There were bi-monthly workshop sessions and there was an element of mentoring. But most importantly, the writers, working in small groups, meeting face to face or using email, analysed other poets among themselves and discussed various poetic concerns. It's a luxury to study (rather than simply read) other poets, and to be obliged to find time to read secondary texts. And it's unusual to study as fellow-practitioners, with the aim of furthering our own creative endeavour rather than to pass an exam. That is what the School principally offered: the obligation to work on our own reading and writing, and the opportunity to share our discoveries with others – practising writers who would provide the kind of specific feedback which illuminates wider issues.

The course to a large extent was designed by the poets themselves, and certainly ran in such as way that it could respond to individual needs. This is partly why, despite a growing collective sense of purpose, each writer was able to remain very much themselves (only more so). Naturally, the School has principles and convictions it holds to; one of these is that we each develop in our own often idiosyncratic way. Each of us will if we're lucky get from A to B but it will be at our own pace and sometimes via Z, or even an entirely different alphabet.

It seemed appropriate, after such an intensive period of work, to ask the writers to look closely at one of their own poems and to consider its main features in light of the Writing School experience. The result is a diverse and diverting anthology that is enjoyable in itself, but which we hope will also prove useful to other writers. One thing which comes through almost all of the commentaries is that the group was determined to have fun. There was a real commitment in this first Writing School, a real sense of enthusiasm, and of mutual respect and supportiveness. It was a privilege to work with such a great bunch of people.

Peter Sansom
Janet Fisher
Editors

Sally Baker

MYTHOLMROYD GIANT

His legs stretch down Caldene Avenue,
past the Health Centre to Walkleys Clogs.
He's tattooed with Give Way and No Entry signs.

The river rushes over his back,
pools around the archipelago
of his vertebrae like strong tea.

I cross the bridge of his belt to catch a bus
the length of his arm to the co-op,
lit like a flashy watch on his wrist.

Then past the sigh of traffic tickling his back,
the canal of his throat,
choked with old bike frames, prams,

washing machines and mythical fish.
Workmen are drilling and digging
from shoulder to thigh.

When he wakes suddenly to all this,
sheep fall off his upper arms,
houses and cars scatter.

He rises like a man buried in sand
by his children while he slept on the beach,
or Gulliver, pinned down in a strange land,

or comatose in a hospital bed, intensive care,
waking to pull out pipes and tubes,
coming to, fuzzy and foggy

at the beginning of a new century,
wondering where he's been all this time,
and his life not his own.

Commentary on 'Mytholmroyd Giant'

The starting point for this poem was walking to the Co-op and watching the river from the bridge, which really did look as if it were swirling over an enormous buried spine. I had this idea of a giant, with everything built on top of him, which I extended in my head while I did my shopping. It's funny living in Mytholmroyd and writing poetry, it feels like it should be significant, but it's not, really. So add to this the sense of living somewhere a really great poet came from, and there's very little to show for it, except a blue plaque on the corner of the house where Ted Hughes was born. It's interesting, what shapes us as people and how much of it has to do with our birthplaces and where we come from, and the sense that we are connected to that place, wherever we go, even if we hate it. I wanted to explore the idea of being famous and all the layers that are put on top of that, which you have little control over, like things that are said about you and your life and relationships, and the tat that is built around the myth – myth being part of the poem, as well as part of Mytholmroyd: the myth of a giant who once lived here and who is lying dormant under the ground.

There's something a bit frightening in there because it's partly the sadness of becoming popular, that you are trapped and that your life becomes not your own, entirely, but also there's the fear of him suddenly waking up and discovering all this and being really angry and powerful. This is especially true once someone is dead and can no longer defend themselves or put their side of the story. I dread living somewhere which suddenly becomes a shrine to a dead poet, like Haworth with all the Bronte tea shops and gift shops. Hebden Bridge is bad enough as it is. One of the refreshing things about Mytholmroyd is how unaffected it is, how real. But now that there's going to be a Ted Hughes Centre, who knows what it will be like? Soon all the cafes will be renamed Ted's Plaice and gift shops will open up, selling collectable fluffy toy badgers and foxes and tea towels with his poems printed on them.

First Draft:

The river rushes over his back,
pools around the islands
of his vertebrae like strong tea.
His legs stretch down Caldene Avenue,
past the health centre to Walkleys Clogs.
He's tattooed with Give Way and No Entry signs.
I cross his belt to catch a bus
along the length of an arm to the co-op,
lit like a flashy watch on his wrist.
Workmen are drilling and digging all over his body.
He's patched and repaired,
                propped up on a hillside to mind sheep.

The first draft fizzled out because I hadn't taken it far enough. At this stage I had some help from my OCA tutor, who pointed out it was a good idea that needed developing. This first version has the giant tamed and given a job to keep him occupied, like a retired old man. The giant's power had not been allowed out. It's quite common for me to lose energy for a poem halfway through. I might start with an interesting idea then not really know where to take it or how to resolve it. Sometimes it can be a real effort to push through this , and I resent having to do the work required. I started to think about other giants and the idea of Gulliver was most obvious as a great man who'd been pinned down by small men. There was also that idea of being buried in sand by children; being weakened by sleep or illness. At some point it fell into three-line stanzas, with a bit of shifting here and there. I like three-line stanzas and often use them, although I might shift form back and forth while I'm drafting to make sure it really works and is not just a habit I've got into.

The version I took to the Writing School course day was somewhere between the two drafts. I had arrived where I wanted to be but needed help with further refinements and tightening up. I like the workshop environment for this fine-tuning, especially when people aren't afraid of making critical comments. This is particularly helpful for getting rid of really naf lines or clichés I might have missed (this version had the line 'After dark he roars at the moon' which was promptly struck out) and also for grammar and form, which I'm not always very good at but which has a lot of impact on the strength of a poem. It's also a good way to test out a poem to see whether it works in terms of being understandable and doing what you want it to do. Some of my poems I had thought were blatantly obvious have baffled whole groups of people. Changing the first lines around was suggested to make a stronger start, which I think works well.

The last line was important to the poem because it's key to the idea of who or what we belong to, not just famous people whose work, or life even, become public property, but ordinary men and women whose lives are taken over by repetitive or dissatisfying jobs, ill health and the quest for gold and possessions, like the flashy watch in the poem, while all the time their throats are choked up with rusty things, things from childhood and stories that are covered over with gloss and tea towels.

Susan Burns

FRIDAY NIGHT AT THE TRAVELLERS

After a week of non-stop work and slow driving
you're in a mood to see some friends.
You're in a mood for a miracle story.

If you could hear yourself think in here
you'd remember that Muslim lad last week –
painted nails, ankle bells
and the bruise of a henna tattoo
on his arm that translates as
I AM A MESSENGER FROM GOD –
who looked at you in all sweet seriousness,
said *I would like to sit down with you,*
take a camomile tea.

You read that the wounds of the stigmatics
gave forth a perfume. So could not be fake.

Just as Sean's telling you about his day,
back from burying his brother-in-law:
Teddy Boy. Club foot. Zephyr 6.
Always called him *Raddish*
on account of his red face:
wasn't so funny when he married your sister.

In any group of more than three
you'll find a critic, a realist, a visionary.
If only.

Wrap yourself around the menu.
Don't flummox the It-girl by changing your order.
Soon, there'll be toothpicks, the bill to settle
and six in the taxi going home.

Commentary on 'Friday Night At The Travellers'

Some days the whole of living
is like a phrase you overheard in the subway
and didn't quite believe –

I love this, the opening line from John Ash's 'Romanza'. Sometimes you read something and you say to yourself yes, that's what it's like, that's my experience too: that sparky thrill of recognition. I discovered this poem (from *Disbelief*) some time after I wrote 'Friday Night at the Travellers' so I can't pretend it inspired it, but the poem, and the whole of the book, did help in the writing about it. This line became a sort of affirmation. It gave me permission, if you like, to stick with a poem which was always in danger of collapsing for lack of being about a solid subject matter but which, now I look back on it, is about the experience of overhearing, or just about the extraordinary things people sometimes say to you in the ordinary course of a week. If you're the sort of person people say things to, which I am.

This is a poem about Friday night. There's nothing like a deadline to concentrate the mind and having to produce a poem for a Saturday workshop often found me fumbling around on a Friday night for a completed piece of work. This was written on one such occasion, towards the end of summer 2003. I had always wanted to write a poem about Friday night. In the June of that year we had taken the children to Glastonbury and on the Friday night the headline act was David Gray (an artist I'd never paid much attention to although we have his CDs in our collection) and to open he sang 'Babylon', which begins:

Friday night I'm going nowhere, all the lights are changing green to red

and which struck me at that time, on that hillside, as the best opening line of any song ever. You had to be there. The mention of slow driving early on refers to my shameful nine points for speeding. This is my twenty-eight-miles-an-hour-in-third-gear poem. I like to think of it like that, like the traffic lights in the song. So the Friday night of the title and the mention of slow driving are for David Gray. Not that anyone needs to know that.

The poem comprises a soundtrack of a week and what I can only own up to as thief poetry. Maybe the compression of someone's life into six words (Teddy Boy. Club Foot. Zephyr 6) and an anecdote is more obituary than poetry, but I love the economy and humour in everyday working-class gossip. So maybe I'm not entitled. But that's how poetry, like love, makes me feel – like a bystander.

I wrote the poem late one night after an evening out at the end of a week in which I was, amongst other things, the continuity girl on a film that included a scene where a tattoo miraculously appears on the hero's arm. Rather that was in the script (by Anna Zaluczkowska and very good too), but we forgot to film it. I blame the continuity department. So, I thought I'd restore it in a poem. I'd also been reading about Catholic imagery. Friday night is crucifixion night, and I'd been wondering whether the stigmatics were simply early self-harmers or whether bleeding wounds really did appear on the hands and feet of the saints.

The composition of the poem rushed into my head at the moment I heard about the guy who died and for me that story and the cruelty of the nickname, somehow connected to religious fervour, to the filming and to some rather odd encounters I had during the week. It came to me apiece, in two parts – the henna tattoo part and the Raddish part. When I got home, I typed it up straight onto the computer screen. (Later still, I lost it in a computer crash and I hadn't kept a paper copy. I remembered it though, almost word for word.)

I don't often go to the pub on a Friday night, or any night. Moreover, this pub isn't exactly a pub any more. It has become one of those gastro places, run by a glamorous woman known locally as the It-girl. I tried to work in a description of the pub as a church, or a cave or a shrine, but I left all that out – metaphor just doesn't do sometimes. Not when they are so obvious. I wanted it – the poem not the pub – to be an incantation to Friday nights, the night when the contents of the week unravel and you try to make sense of it all, or to forget it.

Some of us women in the Writing School had talked in the corridor about gender difference: how men have the confidence, the belief, to write things in poems as if they were so. I wanted, for the sisters, to write a poem consisting entirely of maxims, a sort of kickass manifesto in praise of the versatility of floral wellingtons or something. I never managed it, but here there's one maxim, an example of the sort of new-age management bollocks that passes for abstract thought and of which you hear a lot around here. In fact I did overhear someone (myself?) spouting this theory that very week:

> In any group of more than three,
> you'll find a critic, a realist, a visionary.

I didn't overhear a jingle of course, but here I use rhyme to make it sound ridiculous. I have a weakness for rhyme though like nicotine I long to give it up or at least to cut down. Although my then aged 10 daughter's comment when I embarked on the Writing School stays with me: *what's the use of poetry if it doesn't rhyme?* Whatever. The addiction is evident here and it certainly rhymes in places: I especially enjoy the rhyming of *stigmatics* with *fake*. There must be a reason for that. I added that bit in much later and could have gone crazy with rhyme – *hysteric/ecstatic* and so on. Other rhymes I try and hide. The last four lines for example has flummox/toothpicks/six/taxi. I realise that this may be one six too many, but at the end of a poem, always the most difficult to write, only the truth will do.

Maybe the poem misses its religious mark and maybe that's the point. It's conversational. It's in everyday language, but with words I enjoy: *miracle, toothpick.* It doesn't have much shape – just the stitching of long and short lines and of things tailing off. The translation in capital letters is meant to shout. I hope the material gives it its own shape. I never feel entirely in control of the material but it's less uneven that it was, thanks to Ann Sansom's email editorial interventions. After all, at the end of the night you pile into a cab and go home, hoping for the best. I hope it's a poem. I never know.

To conclude, my aim in this poem was to connect phrases overheard from the unreal life around me with the halting invitation from the boy, real enough though you didn't quite believe it at the time. Sometimes I think that's what poetry is: hard to believe. Fictional truth. All of life in a week in the synchronicity of the real and the imagined: the tattoo, the It-girl, 'Babylon', the stigmata, the funeral, the speed cameras, being part of a group: all of the things you don't quite trust but which are *the whole of living* or your experience of the truth. And if the poem is less than the sum of its parts then so be it.

Chris Considine

DR FELDHEIM'S CALENDAR

Not visited in his cell by angels but by numbers
in their measured dance, cleaner than deeds
or words, bringing the illusion of sanity.

His paces across concrete, multiples of the five
from corner to corner. His pulse-beats
that quickened at the knockings on the wall.

The intensifications of darkness could be called
nights, and counted. And mathematical conundrums
progressed like constellations through his mind.

Afterwards, in a land that was never home,
he was compelled like the ancient mariner
to recount the insults of his fatherland:

annihilated days and months and years,
the never-existing wife and child. To my father,
the spellbound wedding-guest, he gave

a wooden calendar. Four cubes: numbers to ten
(six doubling as nine), Sonntag to Samstag,
Januar to Dezember. All their permutations.

Tokens of lost time and lives. After his death
faithfully every day my father built the date
as a remembrance. Now he too is dead

I rearrange the scratched and battered blocks
to mark their posthumous days when I remember.

Chris Considine

Commentary on 'Dr Feldheim's Calendar'

In middle age my father became friendly with Heinz Feldheim, a German Jew with whom he often lunched in the part of London where they both worked. My father tended to go on and on about his friends and activities and we tended to switch off. Later I wished I had listened and even made an effort to meet Dr Feldheim, with whom my father kept in touch until Feldheim's death. It was when I read a memoir he had written that I realised how interesting and moving his story was.

  A mathematician, he had been unable to get a job in 1930s Germany because he was a Jew. Then he was imprisoned both in Dachau and in Auschwitz on suspicion of having written anti-Hitler propaganda. Miraculously he was released shortly before the war, emigrated to England and lived and taught there until his retirement.

  The draft which follows (['Untitled']) is a shortened version of my first attempt to write about him. Somehow it was too vague, too weak. I tried again in 'Dr Feldheim's Calendar' (the calendar was a gift to my father from South Germany where HF had retired). I think there is a lot to be said for tying emotions/themes to *things*. The calendar was a concrete way in to the subject. It can also, I think, be offensive to seize on the major traumas of other people just to add interest to *your* writing. Why should *I* presume to touch on the Holocaust? I hoped to legitimise my allusion because of the personal/family connection. 'Dr Feldheim's Calendar' was originally offered to the group with a longer middle line in stanza 6: '(two zeros, ones, twos; six doubling as nine), Sonntag to Samstag.' I personally was interested in exactly what numbers were on the 12 faces of the relevant cubes – two zeroes etc. being the minimum required – but others found this a distraction, and that the 'look' of the poem was spoilt. I also originally had a comma in the last line after 'days'. It was suggested that this was unnecessary and made the last line a bit portentous. I quite like this poem (and I like the title) but I now think the first three stanzas are rather cryptic. The reader has to think hard to work them out.

[UNTITLED]

In solitary confinement
he never saw sunlight
or breathed cleanness.
Nights were black
and days were twilight.

Without clock or watch he knew
the twilights grew longer and longer
then shorter and shorter and colder.
He measured his cell over and over:
five paces from corner to corner.

He paced until the soles of his feet
burned on the concrete
and blood sang in his head.
At first he thought
the knocking was his pulse-beat

but then he understood
other hands were touching
the walls he touched
and his knuckles answered
knocking with knocking.

He learnt powerlessness,
came to believe in fate.
To be or not to be
was not up to him.

Chris Considine

All he could do was wait.

And fate set him free.
He does not try to give
reasons why he was chosen,
before his multitude
of domestic ghosts, to live.

Peter Knaggs

SPIDERLINGS

I wipe the strength
      that is being sapped out of my forehead
with my wrist bone.
         It's taking everything out of me to lift
a yard-full of paving slabs through
      the house.

Here, I just need to shift these quiet bricks
         past the spade
with the snapped handle and the coal bunker,
      in one of those
summer fete buzzer games, careful. I'm winning.

Then. She's there, a small spider. Doesn't scurry.
      She stays, gummed to the brick
in gravity defying obstinate courage, her body
like Prince Rupert's Raindrop, her cardiac mark
      the embossed pattern of a medieval shield.

That thing, that urges her to stay put, transmits the coxa,
trochanter, femur, paella, tibia, relays the metatarsus,
tarsus to the claw. She claws the brick,
    sentry to her hackle-band
        silk cocoon
her egg sac
    and
I curve the brick, in my maroon
        industrial glove
admire the engineering –
the calamistrum valved through the cribellum spigot
    to hitch this skein

into a hammock.

Every instinct telling her to guard
      the development of her progeny
from – this man, so strong he can lift
paving slab after paving slab,
   in his shorts.

The shapes I'm observing, the egg
   of the cocoon
    the egg
   of the carapace, take me
to the pages of the pregnancy and birth books
with their cross section of the womb,
  my wife's tummy
a balloon. It would destroy us were anything
  to happen.
So I shunt a brick forward, sit the spider back,
upside down, in the gap
    and think of my spiderlings spinning
      that piece of parachuting silk
that sees them blown out into the world.

She has given herself to them.
They'll eat her at her funeral

Commentary on 'Spiderlings'

 I picked this poem because the premises I had when I started writing it, the techniques I used and the way I wrote it, sprang from the things I was thinking about after attending The Writing School. Firstly, perhaps it isn't finished yet. Secondly, as an outline, I am attempting a number of things. One is to use my knowledge or that energy that you have when you learn, to impact on the poem. So, I was reading about spiders, hence… Also I wanted to go for it, to trust myself, for the poem to convey energy, so I chose to write free form. Sound is important, so I was looking for cadence and intonation, but if they didn't fall, I didn't want to force them. So I tried this Burnsidian-relaxed line structure.

Apart from that, it's a straight forward description of an occurrence. We have a coal bunker, and I was moving the bricks from the left of it, to the gap between the bunker and the house, to make room for more paving slabs, which I was carrying from the front garden to the back. So, quite a masculine job. At the time, Annabel was pregnant. I lifted a brick and I saw this spider. Now normally when you see a spider they run like chuff, but this spider lurked around her nest of eggs. She wouldn't move. Watching this spider, and thinking about how brave she was, protecting her spiderlings, it really affected me. So, I tried to write about it. Of course spiders aren't brave, it's instinctual isn't it? But nevertheless, that is the story behind the poem.

Re-reading it, the first three lines look a bit ropey. I think I'll take another look at them. It's perhaps worth pointing out that the mother spider stays with the eggs until they hatch and then the baby spiders eat her. So that is the last two lines. I realise that there is a suggestion that Dan (the baby in Annabel's womb) may eat Annabel. I don't want the reader to interpret the poem to mean this, but I do like the end of the poem as it is. I am going to spend a bit of time editing this poem over the next couple of weeks. I'm going to try and bring it under 50 lines, in order to enter it into the BBC Wildlife Poet of the Year Competition. I like the poem and I think I almost approach what I'm capable of, in terms of writing a poem. I'm pleased with the vocabulary, the way I've used my knowledge and that it is reasonably un-influenced. Is this the voice of Peter Knaggs? I think so, I hope so.

What else? Is it true that in every back garden there is a spade with a broken handle?

Kath McKay

MENU DEL DÍA

Booked a hotel with a 'hairdresser' in every room, said hola
to Esteban five times a day on the stairs, but sometimes it was
Tomas, who said Buenas and told us that Chueca, where Pilar lived
was full of hippies and that we should take care. Precauciones.
Scrambled eggs with prawns, hake and salad, ice cream.

Spent longer than I wanted in the bathroom. Fell down a hole
in the street, full of murky black water, trooped up past Esteban,
smelling of drains. Pásate, Pásate, he smiled. Scrubbed off black gunk
with yellow soap that smelled of childhood.
Perfect fried aubergines. Grilled salmon, fried potatoes. Flan.

Wrapped a blanket round me at three in the morning while others
got ready to go out, cars tooted below us and in a doorway two drunks
who were fighting changed it to a kiss. Grave waiters spun bread,
wine and water onto tablecloths. Heard the pad of barefoot nuns.
Broad beans. Hake medallion, fried potatoes. No pudding.

Came in on the maids talking about us hanging clothes on the balcony.
Heard the shouts of Guernica, saw arms flung back, a head, mouth open,
a donkey braying, a piece of the cross. Felt the moth breath of a pickpocket
on Sol. 'Your bag is open, señora', said a woman.
                              Moved everything to the front.
Mixed Salad. Cod. Chips. Yogurt in its supermarket carton.

In the Prado saw Italians cluster round a saint receiving breastmilk
from the Virgin. His mouth opened to a long stream of bright light.
Banners on balconies were 'contra la guerra'. Another Madrid 'es posible'.
Against the noise. *Eight months without sleep. Our children are ill. Justicia.*
Gazpacho. Tuna in tomato sauce. Cheese and crackers at Pilars.

Patatas bravas, pimientos de padrón, gambas a la plancha, tortilla,
                    pizza marinera.

Kath McKay

Commentary on 'Menu del dia'

I wrote 'Menu del día' after going to Madrid in September 03 with my partner and thirteen year old daughter. We stayed in the Plaza Ana, just up from Sol, and every day had to walk the gauntlet of tourist places where waiters stood out in the middle of the road and tried to entice us in for the *menu del día*. The area was full of nightclubs and so noisy that the people who lived there with children were constantly battling for their children's health.

I have always been in love with the sounds of the Spanish language. Brought up on a diet of Hemingway and Spanish lessons in Liverpool, where the teacher (a liar, like many of them) told us that coming from Liverpool we had the perfect accent for speaking Spanish ('gente, garaje, giralda' he gobbed on us), I graduated to reading Lorca while working the till at Butlins for a summer job. The sound of the words on menus is as good a poetry as anything.

September 03 was my first time in Madrid, although I knew a couple of people there and had had a madrileño friend for years. I loved it from the start – the noise, the wired up nature of the people, with even the children having dark circles under their eyes, the straightforward friendliness, the gravity of some, the oddness of seeing beautiful young women with missing limbs begging in the street, the lack of compromise in delivering a convent tour solely in Castilian Spanish.

We stayed in a small hotel with oddly translated facilities. One day I fell down a drain in the street and walked back to the hotel with my white trousers covered in foul smelling oily gunk. Esteban cheerfully waved me in to get a shower, not worrying about the trail of slime I left up the newly cleaned three flights of stairs. I was pickpocketed on Sol, but only my reading glasses taken. This seemed balanced out by the friendly concern of a stranger. And when I finally stood in front of Picasso's 'Guernica', I cried. No reproductions had prepared me for seeing it for real. Others in the gallery had tears in their eyes and, like me, kept circling back through the gallery and round to it again.

But our thirteen year old didn't want to go to museums, and would rather eat at El Corte Ingles than a place the guy in the hotel recommended, run by his mate. Every afternoon, exhausted, we lay down and listened to the street noises outside and watched Spanish cartoons, or soaps where the women had improbable facelifts so that when they quivered with emotion, nothing moved. Every evening we would rouse ourselves, shower and walk the streets, deciding where and what to eat.

I had little solo time and the only writing I managed seemed to consist of lists of foods we had eaten. When I came back to England (with food poisoning – I reckon it was dodgy prawns and warm cream cheese) I noticed again a Spanish Tourist board 'Spain marks' advert, one version which has a picture of a pilgrim with sunburnt feet showing paler sandal strapmarks. In a Writing School workshop we had been given the title 'What I did on my holidays', so I started with that, with the sub-title 'Menu del dia'. I began with a line adapted from the advert: 'Madrid marks', and started on about food poisoning and bathrooms and black gunk on my trousers. I love lists (people criticise me for it), so I went back to my lists of foods and started to incorporate them. I wanted to get that feeling of the mundane everyday nature of our trip, with a sense of melancholy and sadness which never seemed very far away in Madrid.

I usually get at least one poem from a trip away. This time I thought I wouldn't get any. I came back ill, tense and out of sorts and had to go to my sister's for a weekend to recover. I took a train out to the seaside and sat alone by the North Sea. Gradually the poem began to come. I cut and cut until it felt harder and sparer. I lost confidence at one point. How can you get the feel of a place in a week?

I took this poem to the Writing School in November. I don't know if people were just being kind to me, or if they genuinely liked the poem, but I got very little feedback. One person suggested I miss out the 'What I did on my holidays' of the title and just went with 'Menu del día'. Someone liked the 'yellow soap that smelled of childhood'. One person asked what 'Pásate' meant, someone else said the poem made them hungry. Another liked the 'moth breath of a pickpocket.'

The poem isn't exactly as I'd like it. The rhythm feels a little skewed at times. Yet it will have to stay as it is at the moment, imperfect until I get the energy to re-do it. For me, it's a record of a particular week in autumn 2003. Places and people leave a body memory.

Paul Mills

THE PRESIDENT OF ENGLAND

The day you woke up unable to find words,
only repeat, What's going on dad?
I took you first to the doctor who said cannabis
could have got through the membrane softened
by meningitis exhaustion into your brain,
that it would pass (maybe)
then having tried all day to bring you out of it
drove you that afternoon to the A & E.
Could you count back from 100 in 3s? (you could).
Did this mean you would be granted asylum
in the land of the sane?
Not necessarily, we would have to wait.
And who is the President of England?
asked the locum, a young German, handsome
and with a still-concerned nonchalance when we laughed,
and a am-I-supposed-to-know-these-things smile.
Come again, you said to him, get real!
So we pronounced you *you* and brought you home.
Two days later your mind slipped from its ledge
down, down. We took you in, screaming for life,
for your newly emerged adult life,
twisting and furious. This is the only way
you'll get it back, I shouted, delivering you
to the doctors for days, maybe for weeks, for life.
It was your twenty first birthday.
In just days the Presidents of England and America
launched their attack and search, while the terrorist
hidden in his folded mountain cave
kept to himself the map and the legend.

Paul Mills

Commentary on 'The President of England'

This poem was one of the first to be written in a sequence of twenty one poems (at the latest count) on the subject of a short but intense period of mental illness suffered by my daughter in the autumn of 2001. The bulk of the sequence was written during the time of the Writing School, beginning the following July. This sequence came to be known among those who offered comments as the 'Lucy poems', a convenient label but misleading in that, apart from her name, the Lucy of Wordworth ('She dwelt among the untrodden ways ... a maid whom there were none to praise and very few to love') bares no resemblance whatsoever to this one, and could hardly be more opposite. The only connection lies with the speaker's intimations – his fear of imminent loss, and state of shock.

To read this poem (so I imagine) creates the impression that the writer isn't making anything up. This (he says) is what happened, more or less. A tendency in some recent contemporary poems is to write as if the speaker tells about events that could be real or fictional – which, we can't be sure; the boundaries are erased. In 'The President of England', the speaker speaks, and acts, without such easy escape routes or audience-calming measures. During a discussion of the poem at one of the Writing School sessions no one raised any objection to its strongly autobiographical subject matter except to say that maybe it was a mistake to use such a localised reference as the invasion of Afghanistan – something that perhaps would in time lose its significance. I made no changes to this however. On the autobiographical issue I'm aware that, especially when writing about anything as complex as mental illness, the gain in specificity can only be achieved at the expense of privacy. A writer would know nothing about it in that amount of detail – or feel its impact with that intensity – unless it had happened to them or their close relatives. What then follows is a problem of disguise, displacement or evasion, but in certain circumstances it might be possible, especially when the story itself is so vivid, to put strategies aside and just get on with telling it as it is.

Even so, what is the story here? Any telling surely involves distortion. If the illness itself demonstrates distortion, who will restore order, supply perspective and predict an outcome? In the poem the speaker is placing a lot of trust in doctors and psychiatrists. The question his daughter first puts to him – 'What's going on?' – he automatically re-addresses to them. Perhaps this is what most of us would do. But of course there's no answer, or only one that by the end of the poem lies with the word 'terrorist' – that is: threat and uncertainty.

Since her period of illness corresponded closely with the unfolding sequence of major events beginning with 9/11, the fact that I associated these with our own private experience was probably inevitable. Both appeared completely out of nowhere and changed everything. Both pointed out the fragility of things previously assumed to be wholly secure. 'What's going on?' – the question regularly popping up in the middle of average TV soap-opera scripts, applies to the mind and to the human future. The story in each case is a struggle to find out what the story is, (will we, can we, ever be certain?) possibly also the struggle to avoid knowing. The story of the poem's composition may be equally precarious. So much depends on the comment by that locum in that hospital. Had he asked 'Who is the Prime Minister…?' the logic of suggestion would never have triggered those last lines.

The link between mental illness and art expression is too huge a subject for this short commentary, but one common symptom might be that a sense of proportion has been lost, and that this loss is deliberate and creative (for the artist), or pathological. In some cases it could be both. The artist sheds the prescriptions of normal thinking, gets interested in other connections, in images, in the unconscious, in disproportion, while the patient suffers these things involuntarily and resorts to patterns of behaviour closer to childhood, has to relearn the coded language of adult interactions – most of which most of us take for granted. The fluid exchange between world and mind has somehow ceased to operate, and speech distortion becomes one of the first recognisable signs that this has happened. The phrase `get real` obviously refers to forms of distortion that stop a person from being in the same kind of world as everybody else. So when the patient tells the doctor `get real` – and we share her view – we take this as proof of recovery of proportion, of the fact that hospitals are no longer necessary in her case – untrue, as it turned out. The tone of the poem helps this humour along – the sense that we can understand proportion and disproportion and can enjoy the difference. The comic tone seems to me a vital element here, making the poem sociable to its readers. It shows how this bonding works between the people in poem, then how it collapses.

The poem-sequence goes on to record rapid recovery, but whether the `story` can ever be recovered – one replete with explanations, causes and effects – is another thing. Writers know their limitations, as do psychiatrists – or one hopes they do. Lucy recovers, but the world does not, and seems instead to have amplified the disaster. As a friend commented after reading the sequence: `The larger neurosis in the public world is evoked as an appropriate context for the private disaster – though the personal crisis resolves itself in a way the public one has not yet done. (I was surprised to recognise references to the public world in 25% of the poems) `. I was surprised too. The references to it in `The President of England` amount to a lot more than 25% but I still think the poem gets it right – the right balance. It seems to me a poem that is both personal and public and sociable – the kind I wish I`d written more of.

Jane Routh

THE RIVER PILOT'S WIFE

Come up the embankment: this is where
she would have watched for ships with a pilot's flag.

Look, back there, that's Read's Island, where he'd show her
the mandarin ducks' nest. Every spring as long as she can remember

lifting her to the bank to keep her skirts dry. Bending the reeds
for her to see. She always knew she would marry Isaac.

He'd row over to Paull to fetch her boiled shrimps. Maud stole
copper nails for him in her apron pocket from her father's yard.

Her girl's pride whenever she picked out a white-and-red flag
on a ship in Brough Roads. She was 15 when he kissed her.

Imagine her two months married and walking up here as if to meet him.
She can count on one hand the nights he has spent in her bed.

Just before dusk, like now, she hears the whistles and groans of waders
among the skypools and purple shadows on the mudflats

and she hears again his mothers' warnings: truant on that raft in the creek,
never a dry garment on him, out all day and out all night;

his own stories of current and tide, captains looking out for him,
and that leap from the deck, in the wind, in the dark: that leap.

She knows her own nights and days now governed by moons,
                                                                    her own tide
turned, that flood of expectation now ebb and the fear of loss

and as she stares into the night, it seems to her that every star
                                                                    and its reflection
is signalling intemperate demands for a pilot to come on board.

Jane Routh

Commentary on 'The River Pilot's Wife'

A poem about a woman married to a Humber Pilot was on my mind for several weeks before I wrote anything. I looked at maps of the Humber, read up on wildlife along its shores and about the nineteenth century Hull fishing industry; I checked the light and flag signals for pilot boats and digressed into the Humber Pilots' dispute with Associated British Ports. By chance, a walk at the mouth of the Lune Estuary reminded me of what mudflats look like in evening light.

I re-read translations of Li Po's 'The River Captain's Wife' including Pound's. (I used the idea of sharing food – but exchanged Li Po's plums for shrimps, as I'd read about Paull shrimping boats a couple of years ago. The mandarin ducks gesture at Li Po: they're a Chinese symbol of fidelity.)

To believe in this woman, I imagined her conversations, brothers and sisters, her hair, the view from her window, her own children. Little of this is left in what I wrote (though stanza 8 comes from an imagined conversation between Maud and Isaac's mother). It has to do its work like Tom Phillips's *Drawing: A Film*, in which – although every mark is erased – some ghostly trace of what was nevertheless seems to remain.

This is the pleasurable part of writing: everything is still possible. So is that first rush of ideas and phrases that spill on to the page. After this, I'm *outside* the poem and there's no going back in. The work is no longer about collecting, but about stripping away and shaping.

I don't always work like this. But I *am* always concerned to open up this sort of poem as something that has been constructed. In earlier drafts, I tried phrases like: 'Whether I met her when I was a child I'm not sure'. In the end I use a direct address to the implied reader: the opening 'Come' and the second stanza's 'Look'. The conditional tense underlines the suppositions. 'Imagine her' in the middle stanza (which marks a shift into 'her' present tense) invites the reader into this invention, although what is to be imagined is of course specified: 'two months married and walking up here as if to meet him'.

One or two undulating phrases in my first notes felt right for a poem about the sea that doesn't actually have events in it: they determined the long-lined couplets. Stanzas 2 and 3 needed most work: their phrases were broken and re-arranged into this form, until 'lifting her' opened a stanza and seemed in turn to lift the poem.

This is a not-quite-there-yet version of the poem, the version to leave and come back to afresh months later. The penultimate stanza needs those 'now's tidying. Ann Sansom's suggestion of 'have a think about where the name Maud comes in' might lead either to dropping the name altogether, or using it earlier. I've already revised the last line thanks to Ann and taken out 'intemperate' because – as she says – it 'feels more urgent if shorter.' Paul Mills wants it in though: 'I think this poem needs more sense of your presence moving around with the characters, commenting implicitly. I think the ending of the poem – especially the last line and the word 'intemperate' is a kind of comment – the right kind, just a touch of the finger in the scale'.

What to do will seem obvious only after I've left the poem alone for a while.

Ann Sansom

ST. AUGUSTINE'S HOUSE

Star of the Day all afternoon for bursting head down through the line,
the remains of the relay team gone mad on the far side of the track.
Well done, St. Augustines. Team effort, team spirit. Not mine, then.
Not even when I come coasting in off the sprint, eyes shut, hands up.

Even the man who lands every week with a suitcase full of bagpipes –
ignore him, girls - pauses in his slow adjustments. Even Sister Sebastion
wants to smile. It's fifty merit points to St. Augustine's House, my house.
It might redeem the end of term disgrace. It never does. Lost cause,
                                                            won race.

So this – *you will not run in corridors, you will not ever raise your voice* –
is my own not quite controlled explosion, my private celebration
of the mastery of the thigh and heart and inflamed throat.
                                        No need for style
or grace or piety when you're invisible, so quick you don't exist as flesh,

until you sink into the grass with something vast and small,
                                        intangible and grasped
and loaned and kept. Well done. A minute's pleasure calling back
                                        the breath
well spent in service to a form of indolence, a minute's peace,
                                                a coming to,
before – not yet – the Honour Shield to St. Augustine's hopeless house.

Ann Sansom

Commentary on 'St. Augustine's House'

Sometimes I think that some poems turn up more or less intact. Not enough sleep, a long period of concentrated reading, Mercury changing direction, Jamesons, a new biro – who knows how these things arise – but somehow they do, almost effortlessly, needing few if any adjustments. A gift.

And I go on believing this puerile nonsense, in fact preaching it, until I'm faced with my earlier drafts, which generally bear only a Hapsburg resemblance to the version I thought I'd had from the off. This delusion was exploded, not for the first time, but most resoundingly when I e-mailed what I believed to be an early draft of a newish poem – not this one – to Susan Burns. It was still a bit gobshitey and not ordered right, but she's a friend, and wouldn't shoot it down on sight (*'your new baby looks very simian to me.'*) I knew that poem was awkward and I hadn't quite got the hang of it, but I thought it might come to something later.

I was appalled when she responded – positively – but, somewhat burdened by the huge document she'd been obliged to scroll through and take to work in a carrier bag. *Get back to you soon,* she said.

Appalled. In the 8am bathroom sense. 23 full pages, when I checked. And every one ricocheting between the original version via a series of worthless showy adventures into something approaching coherence. What a shameful morning that was. Like waking up remembering how you'd bent someone's ear in the early hours. (*'I have poisoned a poet by talking too much.'* – *Lydia Tomkiw*). Enough. She understood. And I gave up again on the gift fallacy.

I'm not suggesting for a second that I slave over the craft. Have sense. Just that I operate a selective amnesia; lopping out my more lunatic departures.

Some writers, I know, won't set down a syllable until they have the whole poem ordered. I admire that no end. To remember a whole poem. And to sort it out internally. No recourse to ink.

Strength of character and disciplined thinking. Capacity.

One line, I can understand that. It hovers, doing not much harm at all, like a fat idling bee, dozing on the window sill until you try to usher it out. But to retain a whole poem in your head until it's worth writing down …

Much like meeting a man in a white crash helmet at night in a subway. I was beside myself, but my son went bolt upright in his buggy and applauded.

So, just to make a complete liar of myself, 'St. Augustine's' arrived more or less as it stands.

Or, in this case, gets to have a lie down in the end. Mainly because I lost it a couple of times and it managed to dodge some of my more corrupting ministrations. Once, the notebook went missing. Fancy that. Disaster. Then it turned up. Disappointment. Then I was persuaded into a posh new computer which lost, or pretended to lose, whatever I most wanted to have a look at this very minute. I didn't know how to access a blank page – once I'd found the note book – and was further hampered by my habit of giving esoteric titles to work which is really called something I don't recognise. You'd not credit the grief I demonstrated over the loss of that bagpiper. Turned out it was called 'Sebastion', when I finally tracked it down. It was an odd interesting possibly working poem when it was lost. Found, it was the one line: *ignore him, girls (quelle wanker* – not included but part of the original. Let that be a lesson to me).

For the purposes of this: I started it in a Writing School, an exercise something to do with music, I think. Henry Shukman's 'Piano Solo'? Perhaps not, but I got a small man adjusting his bagpipes. The rest was no use, but for almost forty years I'd hardly given that man a thought and that made him important to me. Every Tuesday – our sports day – he'd arrive on the Town Fields with his suitcase. Tennis, he'd set up and then patrol the mesh, Hockey, he'd be stationed mid-line, Track events, he'd go the length with us. *Ignore him, girls. Do not look.*

I'd ignored him. And apart from skirl which I don't like the sound of, I'd no language for that performance: cock-a-doodling, skirting us and blind-siding a gang of nuns year after year.

What do you call that brazen kilt-swaying, the leaning back strutting counterpoint to their clacking robes, hearty sandals. Not the remotest memory of any sound, in spite of St. Augustine's *audi partem alteram,* hear the other side.

But not entirely ignored as it turned out. The suitcase was very small and is still visible.

Then, given the Music poem, which I hadn't been able to do, we were invited to write a Sporting piece. Frankly, I can't believe that. Most of us would have been obliged to forge a sick note. So it's most likely untrue. Perhaps we were offered the chance to relive a small physical success? No. Not likely. Either way I'd be livid. I'm not a sporty sort of woman. I can't do lacrosse and you can't make me. Might have been an invitation to write about grass. Anyway, I'd got a loose grip on the bagpiper and the track and the gentleness with which he uncoiled his equipment – not 'uncoiled', restrained (?) subdued(?). If you've ever closely observed a man unpacking a set of bagpipes from a suitcase, you'll know how the legs launch out and splay and have to be fielded, and how that dreadful loose bag has to be elbowed in and clamped before he can set his mouth to the pipe. The relief of that achievement. *Ignore him girls.*

I had *indolence* in there, which I know the meaning of. Sounds like idling but far better in the long run. What I aim for, always.

'Star of the Day' I lifted from my youngest daughter – in Y2 they get a smiley yellow E-sticker. We got a navy felt badge to sew on, an embroidered inscription threaded through a gold crown, *Stella Maris.*

So it seemed reasonable to break the first line on *head down*. And it stayed that way for a while. Quite possibly for 23 pages but I hope not. Anyway, I wanted it quicker. And, against all common sense, the longer lines moved it on. The out of breathness of the last stanzas is appropriate, I think. A bit of stamina fuelled by a caterwaul. Or a skirl. Quite possibly one of the angriest poems I've ever been party to. I would have called it 'Bagpiping' but I'd been pipped.

John Siddique

OTHER PEOPLE'S CHILDREN

He is eight and good at football. His mind
flits blacker and whiter than a magpie
from playstation to plastic sword, chocolate,
internet, to nothing to do, to slamming the ball.
He has a will of iron. Can bend his mother's
and my love for him like plasticine;
when he wears his stick-on tattoos
in the same place on his shoulders as I have mine,
when he calls me 'old chappy,' as we scream
through the air as human aeroplanes
I want so much to show him the world
I know, make it right for him.
Their Dad shows up every now and then,
it blows this family sideways, the guy ropes
twang off their pegs, until morning comes
and the wind dies down, and he goes off again
I begin planting and parenting. Applying constancy
at the thin end of myself. But here is the boy
on a Saturday morning, next to me in bed,
hugging his mother and me together,
blowing at my chest hair.

John Siddique

Commentary on 'Other People's Children'

This poem came about because I wanted to do some writing around the theme of family. In the 21st century the word family means something quite different to what it did 40 or 50 years ago. It is a far more flexible, complicated thing than it once was. Reflecting on my own disparate upbringing I find that some of my friends are my family, as are my lovers. I also feel that my step children are part of my family. This can get very complicated if one should break up with a partner, and the children who through so much effort and time feel like yours suddenly aren't again, but that's a poem I haven't written yet.

In this poem I wanted to write about my girlfriend's 8 year old son. I wanted it to be a comfortable poem, that is, sweet but not over sentimental. It is about something profoundly ordinary. Poets often shy away from sweetness, it's far easier to be cold, reflective, or clever. I do these things too often myself and I guess I wanted this poem to be a bit of an antidote to all that.

It's written as a single verse. I don't know why this is, I tried it as stanzas but something really didn't feel right when it was in that form. I have no explanation for this except that it's an artistic decision.

Here is the second draft of the poem. The first draft exists in my notebook, and it's when I type up that the initial edit takes place.

> He is eight and good at football. His mind
> flits blacker and whiter than a magpie
> from playstation to plastic sword, to chocolate,
> to internet, to nothing to do, to slamming the ball
> He has a will of iron. Can bend his mother's
> and my love for him like plasticine
> He is sweet; when he wears his stick-on tattoos
> in the same place on his shoulders as I have mine,

> when he calls me 'old chappy,' as we scream
> through the air as human aeroplanes
> I want so much to show him the world
> I know, make it right for him. I worry
> and my friend tells me to love the children
> wide and open, the best I can. Their Bio-Dad
> shows up every now and then, it blows this family
> sideways, the guy ropes twang off their pegs,
> until morning comes and the wind dies down,
> when he goes off again. I begin planting
> and parenting again. Applying constancy
> at the thin end of myself. But here is the boy
> on a Saturday morning, next to me in bed,
> hugging his mother and me together,
> blowing at my chest hair.

The first changes I made were to get rid of some of the 'to's' from the third and fourth lines. Doing this helped the rhythm of the piece, but also made the poem more succinct

Then I got rid of the statement 'He is sweet' from the seventh line. 'Show me don't tell me,' is the rule and I break it many times in this version, so I also got rid of :

> I worry
> and my friend tells me to love the children
> wide and open, the best I can.

for exactly the same reason. Here I am spelling out the core of the poem and treating my readers as if they don't understand when the love in the poem is obvious, so out it goes.

I had a lot of help getting this poem straightened out, initially at one of the workshops at the Poetry School, when we had Mimi Khalvati in as a guest for the day. She enjoyed the sweet aspect of it, and that gave me the confidence to forge ahead with it. She also identified the problem with 'to'. I also had help from my friend poet Cherry Smyth who had been working with me on editing a pile of new work, as I was pulling the manuscript together for what is now my first collection.

Next out was the 'Bio-Dad' phrase, which is actually what we call him, but again I think I'm spelling it out too much, so just 'dad' is enough.

I am very proud of the ordinariness of this poem, once I stopped telling the reader how to respond to it. It's strange that I set out to write a poem as simply and as straightforwardly as possible, yet I have had to work very hard for that simplicity. Sometimes when I'm reading Hemingway, and I balk at his clarity, I wonder what the trick is, to just say what something is. At present that is where my exploration lies, learning to write down what's there and not get in its way with cleverness, or being a poet. To record, curate and translate, to be the eye.

Steven Waling

YOU SHOWED US YOUR ROW OF CUPS

Remember Wednesday afternoons
when Anxiety always picked us
for his team at football
out in freezing fields lined up
against uniform walls we stood
like the unbuttered face of white bread
when the captains of houses chose sides
and Confidence picked all the bullies
and the lads in smart new kit
as Brilliance and Future Prosperity
chose boys who built guitars
and paid for school meals
while we shivered with the fat boy
who couldn't run in cheap shorts
and pumps off the market
then teamed up with Captain Anxiety
and nobody thought we could win
least of all us and you agreed,
didn't you, with your long corridors
where we waited outside the Head's room
as the games played on without us
and you showed us, didn't you?

Commentary on 'You Showed Us Your Row Of Cups'

There's an earlier version of this poem in which the last line here is the next-to-last line, and the whole thing is in irregular verses with proper punctuation. I took the advice of the workshop and changed those; and it is better. It's angrier and more direct, quicker too.

Also, in an earlier version, the title was a line in the poem, somewhere near the end. But it made a better title than 'The School of Anxiety', which sounds too much like a Charles Simic title (I was reading *Jackstraws* at the time). That line just stuck its neck out and said, 'use me as the title'.

Those capitalised and personalised abstract nouns, by the way (Anxiety, Confidence, Brilliance and Future Prosperity) are straight steals from Simic. And the mode of the poem, the fact that it is talking to the school, is Kenneth Koch's *New Addresses*: but angrier. Look at those two 'didn't you's', the harshness of 'the unbuttered face of white bread': I was obviously angry at someone when I wrote this…

It also started out in regular verses, probably four lines each. Most of my poems start off in verses of four, three or five lines. Part of the reason for that, I guess, is that it provides a box or grid for the thoughts to gather themselves into while they wait to find the right shape. I can't claim to have started a poem until I can go through the whole thing in one go, and I need a shape or a mould to pour the poem into. Then the poem takes on its own life, and I try to find the shape it wants to be rather than the shape I think it should be. Which sounds like the poem isn't entirely controlled by me; well, I hope it's not, actually. I hope there's room for accidents to come in and change things, even at the last minute.

I'm letting you into a few of the secret decisions this poet makes when writing a poem. I know a few people who can write a poem more or less complete in one go; I'm not one of them. It takes me loads of different versions. Even recently, I changed a word; just because it sounded better. Not all the decisions are conscious though: sometimes a line enters my head and I have to put it in, to see how it works. It might be terrible, or it might send the reader in the wrong direction; but I try it anyway. There's one of those lines in this poem. I put it in because it sounded right, not because I knew what it meant or why it was there. I thought of a reason for it later. Sometimes, like Frank O'Hara, you go on your nerve and trust your instinct.

But there are other things happening. Like where do poems come from and what are they about? Well, they come from my life, and they come from ideas floating round in my head at the time. Like, I had a terrible time at Grammar School. So there's a personal element?

Well yes, but I use the first person plural throughout. This is not a confession. Hopefully, anyone like me (working-class, educated at Grammar School and University) can see something of their own lives here. That feeling that you're not the right sort to succeed, you don't have the right accent, you come from the wrong side of the tracks, you're getting above yourself, aren't you? The Cringe in other words.

Sufferers from the Cringe are always anxious about their status, their self-confidence is lacking so they can compensate by shyness, by snobbery, by arrogance, by inverted snobbery ('Poetry is for clever-dicks, not ordinary gruff Northern blokes like me.') Sufferers of the Cringe include the bloke down the pub who thinks all poetry's sissy and the university-educated poet with a chip on his shoulder eulogising his parents' lack of education. But they never quite get rid of the idea that they are not supposed to be this clever, they are supposed to just get a job in a factory and shut up for the rest of their lives.

Or maybe it's just about being different. Being creative in a non-creative environment. Or not being the self-confident go-getting type who will always rise to the top whoever they are, whatever class they are. Or just not liking sport. Or being excluded from sport because it was all about being a team-member and 'success' on the playing field to go along with 'success' in the exam room.

Those are some of the ideas that were going through my head when I wrote this poem. Probably, though it could be later or before the poem was written, I can't really remember. Maybe those ideas were around in the atmosphere at the time, and I just used them to explain the poem to myself afterwards. I don't like knowing what a poem is about before it's written, and anyway the poem isn't *about* any of those things. It's about picking teams during the Games lesson. Like the fat boys and the seven-stone weaklings, I wasn't picked, or we were picked for the losers. I may even have been a seven-stone weakling.

Oh yes, the personal stuff, the lyric 'I'. It had to get in somewhere, didn't it? But you can't come at a subject direct, not in a poem; too much subject makes a poem top-heavy. It can collapse under its own weight. A poem isn't a sermon. So I put my own story into the poem; you can't keep yourself entirely out of your poems, and why should you want to?

Anyway, I don't know how much all this tells you about the poem. It gives you some background, and says something about what the writer thinks the poem means and about how some of it was written. But once it's finished, it's out there for anyone to read, and they can read the poem how they like. So it's up to you now.

Sue Wood

THE CRAFT OF SPINES

Hot thick June evenings, we step outside
for air or a look at the thin
thumbnail moon with a skirl of bats
over the beech tree. Caught in a pool of light
a hedgehog comes with its shift
of small feet on gravel.

We think we know this one.
Want him to come to the garden
from story-book pages where
he wears panto-dame pinnies
over cauldrons of hot clothes,
stands upright and twinkles
small dull eyes.

We are nothing. He sees only
the roots of our feet, hears
our night rustle beyond
his own coded alarm.

Once I found a blind hedgehog
on our lawn at night,
eyes gummed over in a seal of darkness.
Round he went in a circle that met itself,
a planet's scoop across the ache of space.
The next morning he was gone,
his track an agony of flattened grass.

Now we put out the bowl of milk
which he takes as interruption,
stumbles into it, licks a few milky beads,

stops, gyrates his spines
in a pulse of uncertainty.

We fade away, off his screen.
He searches for slugs and beetles
as if his craft of spines cancels
everything except the night
and the luscious sandalled
feet of snails.

Commentary on 'The Craft of Spines'

I'm not usually an animal poem writer although the world outside my window, which happens to be green and rather leafy, often does get into my writing in terms of imagery. This poem is, of course, in company with such as Larkin's poem on a hedgehog, which, I seem to recall, got cut in two by his lawn mower. His is the urban, if not urbane voice, dealing with the messy inconvenience of nature. I'm a gardener of the kind that allows self-seeding and outposts of wildness. So in our garden I'm aware of how many parallel universes exist, side by side, each bird, insect and plant intent on its own form of survival and dependent on all that surrounds it for this to happen. We are the only onlookers in this complex world.

This poem started its life as a writing exercise in one of the Writing School sessions. The opening lines appeared on the page and remain unchanged. My notes read 'Hedgehogs: live within their circle of spines, shape – pincushion, tastes good baked in clay, visor-head to toe, spines=radar, spines=cancelling out of everything except danger'. When I came to re-work the material, I remembered the blind hedgehog scurrying round and round in a circle, hour after hour. His 'programming' appalled me. The poem won a prize in the Peterloo Poetry Competition.

Cliff Yates

HÔTEL DE L'ANGLETERRE

No thanks I don't want a Sandwich Americana.
I'm turning yellow maybe it's the noodles.
I said what do you think should I start

feeling ill? She said my headache's enough
for both of us. I said what about
my toothache? She said what toothache?

Birds sing in French, *massage energetique*
on a lamppost. What a city, what a language!
I have an owl sandwich, an owl shower.

Man on the Metro with one arm does a crossword
in a pink shirt, two men on crutches
in the same carriage. A convention perhaps.

Picasso knew some strange-looking people.
He's excited and she's looking pretty damn good as well.
Large nude in red armchair, large bather with book.

Two profiles for the price of one
and the hat's the only thing straight.
The hat's not straight.

A boy throws a small cardboard
box at a pigeon. What we need
here's a thousand-piece jigsaw.

Cliff Yates

Commentary on 'Hôtel de l'Angleterre'

We spent a week in Paris during the summer of 2002 and I wrote all kinds of things in my notebook: things we said, things I noticed and things that occurred to me – I wrote on the Metro, in the Picasso museum. Back home I typed up the notes and the work started. I say work, but that makes it sound more deliberate than it is. I go at it in bursts, working on more than one poem at a time so that it doesn't get too intense. Hemingway said you should stop when it's going well and I've proved this the hard way. Work too much on a poem in the early stages, or overwork it at any stage, and it's a dead duck.

'Hôtel de l'Angleterre' is more or less representative of one of the ways I was writing until sometime last year, when I took a breath, turned a corner and came up with 'Lighthouse':

> The lighthouse flickers at the end of the pier.
> We watch it in our red pyjamas.
> Actually neither of us are wearing red pyjamas.
> You're wearing my blue shirt …

and a poem called 'L'Hermitage and a Bird' which, as far as I can tell, turned another corner, taking me off this particular map.

I stumbled across the method of writing 'Hôtel de l'Angleterre' the previous summer on holiday in Whitby, when I was looking for a new way of writing. I had with me the old Penguin translation of Apollinaire by Oliver Bernard which I started reading one afternoon on the beach. I think it's the way Apollinaire uses the line in 'Zone,' the sense of speed and nervous energy. 'Hôtel de l'Angleterre' has shorter lines than 'Zone', and is more self-conscious in its use of line-breaks. There's a tension between the tight 3-line stanza structure and the way in which the poem leap-frogs from subject to subject. The voice of the poem, or rather voices, is eager and enthusiastic (me on a good day), plenty to say and no need to fill in the gaps. It trusts the reader.

I'm not so keen on poems that hit you over the head with meaning. I prefer poems that allow me space and leave me something to do. In fact, 'Hôtel de l'Angleterre' appears preoccupied with the possibility of meaning, with making sense and not making sense: the owl joke, the strange skin symptoms and 'A convention perhaps'. Also, 'Picasso knew some strange-looking people' which deliberately misses 'the point'. It isn't only who or what Picasso is painting, it's how he paints it. Same with a poem. Frank O'Hara said about 'Second Avenue': 'I hope the poem to be the subject, not just about it.'

It took me a while to arrive at the title. I thought of calling it by the name of the hotel in which we stayed, but that was Hôtel Style which sounds like the title of an over-earnest collection of poems that I would hate to read. I decided on 'Hôtel Angleterre' and subsequently discovered, from the Rough Guide, that there actually is an Hôtel de l'Angleterre. It was formerly the British Embassy. Hemingway stayed in Room 14.

NOTES ON CONTRIBUTORS

Sally Baker lives in West Yorkshire where she works as an illustrator and gardener. She has had poems in various magazines and collections. Her poem 'Fake Leopardskin Coat' was shortlisted for the Forward (Best Poem) Prize.

Susan Burns runs Chol Theatre, based in Huddersfield, producing community and professional plays and video. She was formerly a Director of the Arvon Centre at Lumb Bank. She lives in Mytholmroyd with her husband and their two children.

Chris Considine. Formerly a schoolteacher in Bedford, she now lives in Swaledale, North Yorkshire. Her pamphlet, *Swaledale Sketchbook*, a winner in the Poetry Business Book & Pamphlet Competition 2001, was shortlisted for the Forward (First Collection) Prize. Her first full collection, *Learning to Look*, was published by Peterloo Poets in 2003. Her next is due in 2005.

Peter Knaggs lives with his wife and two children in Hull, where he works in a bookshop. His poems can be found in the books *Half a Pint of Tristram Shandy*, *Cowboy Hat* and *Shakespeare Ate My Sonnet*. He produces the magazine *The Slab*.

Paul Mill's latest book of poems, *Dinosaur Point*, won the Poetry Business Book & Pamphlet Competition in 1999. Before that, his most recent book was *Half Moon Bay*, published by Carcanet Press. His book for students, *The Routledge Creative Writing Coursebook*, is forthcoming in 2005. He was Gregory Fellow in Poetry at Leeds University and since 1980 he has taught literature and creative writing at York St John College in York.

Kath McKay was born in Liverpool, lived in Hackney for several years, and now lives in Leeds. She's a fiction writer as well as a poet. Her first poetry collection, *Anyone Left Standing*, won the Poetry Business Book & Pamphlet Competition. She teaches creative writing and is an online mentor for Crossing Borders, tutoring writers based in Africa. She gained an Arts Council Award for short stories in 2004. Recently she has been part of Interland, a Yorkshire/Ostrobothnian (Finnish) collaboration, working on a water anthology. She is also writing on the subject of teeth, working with a visual artist producing etchings.

Jane Routh's first full collection, *Circumnavigation*, won the Poetry Business Book and Pamphlet Competition in 2002, and was shortlisted for the Forward (First Collection) Prize. She is also a photographer, and manages ancient woodlands and a flock of geese in the Forest of Bowland, North Lancashire.

Ann Sansom has published two full collections with Bloodaxe: *Romance* and *In Praise of Men and other people*. She is a playwright and producer, and works throughout the country as a writing tutor in schools and with adults. She has gained much recognition for her work, including an Arts Council Award.

John Siddique's first full collection *The Prize* is due from The Rialto in 2005. His work has appeared in numerous anthologies and magazines. He has held residencies at Ilkley and Ledbury Festivals, been Writer in Residence at Wetherby Prison, and is currently Commonword's Poet in Residence.

Steven Waling lives and works in Manchester. He has had several collections published, including *Calling Myself On The Phone* (Smith/Doorstop 2003). He has participated in artistic collaborations at the Lowry Centre, Salford, and Rochdale Art Gallery. He has recently worked with African writers on the 'Crossing Borders' project set up jointly between the British Council and Lancaster University.

Sue Wood has lived in Halifax, West Yorkshire, for the past twenty years and is just beginning to feel at home. Previously she taught in South Africa and contributed her poetry to local journals. She always feels that she is about to become a 'real' poet but the goal posts keep moving, or the garden or running a bed and breakfast take precedence. Her pamphlet *Woman Scouring A Pot* was a winner in the Poetry Business Book & Pamphlet Competition, and she has had poems widely published in good magazines. She also writes and publishes short stories.

Cliff Yates is the author of *Emergency Rations* (2004), and *Henry's Clock* (1999), which won the Poetry Business Book & Pamphlet Competition and the Aldeburgh Poetry Festival Prize. During his time as Poetry Society poet-in-residence he wrote *Jumpstart: Poetry in the Secondary School*. He teaches at Maharishi School where his students are extraordinarily successful at winning poetry competitions. He has received an Arts Council England Writer's Award.